WILLIAM WORDSWORTH
A Lakeland Anthology

To Gum
from Hannah
x x

WILLIAM WORDSWORTH

A Lakeland Anthology

Selected and Illustrated by Piers Browne

Foreword by John Mortimer

John Murray
in association with The Shorthorn Press

I would like to thank those who subscribed to the original, handmade limited edition of this book when it was first conceived in 1988:

John Winter
David and Mary Johnson
Richard and Jane Hall
David Shannon Wright
Edward and Elizabeth Guinness
Malcolm and Josephine Scott
Ian and Susan Purslow
Massimo and Juliet Brooke
Ralph Congreve
Richard and Rachel Boulton

I dedicate this book to them, for without their support it would not have seen the light of day.

This edition is a reproduction of number 1 of the limited edition.

©This selection: Piers Browne
© Illustrations: Piers Browne

Designed by Philip Abel and hand set in Monotype Bembo

First published in this edition in 1991
by John Murray (Publishers) Ltd, 50 Albemarle Street, London W1X 4BD
in association with The Shorthorn Press

BRITISH LIBRARY CATALOGUING-IN-PUBLICATION DATA
Wordsworth, William
  Wordsworth: A Lakeland Anthology.
  I. Title II. Browne, Piers
  821
  ISBN 0-7195-5003-3

Printed and bound in Italy by Graphicom

CONTENTS

Acknowledgements   page viii

Preface   ix

Foreword by John Mortimer   xi

'Was it for this'   1
The Prelude · Book I · Introduction · 1850

Nutting   4
1798-9

'And in the frosty season'   7
The Prelude · Book I · Childhood and school-time · 1850

'One Christmas time'   9
The Prelude · Book XI · Imagination · 1805-6

'One summer evening (led by her)'   12
The Prelude · Book I · Childhood and school-time · 1850

'Mid a throng of maids'   15
The Prelude · Book IV · Summer vacation · 1850

'It was a summer's night'   16
The Prelude · Book XIII · Conclusion · 1805-6

'I travelled among unknown men'   18
1801

Lines composed a few miles above Tintern Abbey   19
1798

Animal tranquility and decay   25
1798

'A slumber did my spirit seal'   25
1800

'She dwelt among the untrodden ways'   26
1799

A Complaint 27
1806

'I wandered lonely as a cloud' 28
1804

'Brook! whose society the Poet seeks' 30
1806

To sleep 31
1807

'The world is too much with us' 32
1807

'From Bolton's old monastic tower' 33
The White Doe of Rylstone · from Canto 1 · 1807-8

'Surprised by joy' 35
1812

A Wren's Nest 36
1833

September, 1815 42
1815

At Furness Abbey 43
1845

Intimations of Immortality 44
1803-6

To My Sister 53
1798

November 1 55
1815

Gordale 56
1818

November, 1836 58
1836

'Strange fits of passion have I known' 59
1799

'There was a Boy'   61
  The Prelude · Book V · Books · 1850

London, 1802   63
  1802

Composed by the side of Grasmere Lake   64
  1807

'On Man, on Nature, and on Human Life'   66
  The Excursion · Preface · 1814

To a Skylark   70
  1825

'O Friend, few happier moments have been mine'   71
  The Prelude · Book X · Residence in France · 1805

Resolution and Independence   73
  1802

Michael   79
  1800

After-Thought   95
  1820

Map   96
List and Location of Illustrations   97

ACKNOWLEDGEMENTS

IN making this selection of Wordsworth's poetry I was helped by Richard and Rachel Boulton who balanced my instinct towards selecting poems for their pictorial qualities alone. In turning the selection, once made, into a book, I acknowledge with gratitude the two years' work of Philip Abel at Hand & Eye. The original edition owes much of its character to his beautiful typesetting and printing, and his successful efforts at restraining my persistent urge to over-embellish the pages. My thanks go also to Alan Tinley for helping me to edition some of the etchings, a number of which were printed off steel kindly supplied by Richard Hall. Moving out of doors away from printers and studio, I must acknowledge the debt that I owe to the late Alfred Wainwright who died aged 84 last January and whose works have made fell-walking so much easier for so many. He once said there was no art in walking, except to look where you are going. With his guidance, I looked where I went and I have illustrated this book with what I saw. It is my hope that these pictures will have a chance to lift the spirits of those who see them, just as his were lifted when he surveyed the sunrise from a fell-top and said 'I feel like a king'.

PREFACE

THE poems in this selection are those in which, I believe, Wordsworth best reacts to small objects of natural beauty with large ideas. Striding at two thousand feet above sea-level he admires the hare's tail cottongrass growing in peat; out bird-nesting on a long walk he finds a wren's nest delightfully hidden by a primrose (page 36). In the first five stanzas of *Resolution and Independence* (page 73), he fills the air with the birdsong of 'a sweet voiced' stock dove, 'an answering' jay, 'chattering' magpie and 'warbling' skylark.

But the catalogues of natural phenomena and accounts of people in Wordsworth's poems are just the starting point. The more awed he is by nature (he is 'led by her' on page 12) the deeper he dives into his imagination. The largeness of his ideas wells up, too, from deep reservoirs of compassion, a trait in his thoughts and imagination which I find deeply appealing. *Resolution and Independence* continues with his climbing to the moorland heights where he is seized by melancholia; but an encounter with an old leech gatherer overwhelms him with a sense of the supernatural, and his spirits revive. These reversals of feeling are explained in a letter which accompanied a pre-publication copy of the poem sent to friends: '. . . this I can confidently affirm, that though I believe God has given me a strong imagination, I cannot conceive a figure more impressive than that of an old man like this, the survivor of a wife and ten children, travelling alone among the mountains and all lonely places, carrying with him his own fortitude, and the necessities which an unjust state of society has laid upon him.'

His conclusion to *The Prelude* seems to me to offer enduring advice for the artist and all humankind:

Imagination having been our theme,
So also hath that intellectual Love,
For they are each in each, and cannot stand
Dividually. -Here must thou be, O Man!
Power to thyself.

As an artist I cannot help but admire a man who, at the age of thirty, returned to his roots to what was considered wild countryside, and who then through his writing did perhaps more than anyone to convert the prevailing idea that those surroundings were a wilderness into a popular appreciation of their virtues as an attractive landscape. It was an artist, Thomas Smith of Derby, who had led the way in 1761 when he published an extremely popular series of Lakeland etchings. Following nearly a decade later came the poet and scholar Thomas Gray, who much appreciated what now became known fashionably as the Picturesque. From 1800, when he settled at Dove Cottage, until his death in 1850 at nearby Rydal Mount, Wordsworth laboured to widen and secure a safe passage for all to the admiration of such beauty. But it is his efforts to transfigure beauty seen with the eye into a universal idea, into something truly sublime, that for me makes Wordsworth a great poet and one who, as an artist, I am unable to equal with my brush and etching needle. It is for you to judge whether the etchings in this book abet Wordsworth in his desire to see 'Fair trains of imagery before me rise'.

FOREWORD
by John Mortimer

ANYONE walking through these landscapes in the early years of the last century might have seen an angular, beak-nosed, untidy figure, carrying an umbrella against the rain, pacing up and down an imaginary cage, perhaps half a mile long. If approached closely he might be heard intoning the finest verse since Milton and Shakespeare, verse not used for heroic or religious purposes but to describe the deep emotions excited by everyday sights and sounds, the towering mountains and waterfalls, a single lovely tree or shepherd's cottage. It was Wordsworth's way to compose poetry in his head, to learn his verses as he wrote them and carry them home in triumph to his sister Dorothy, to Coleridge, to his wife and friends. So his poety was not only about the countryside, but was made there, which may be why he penetrates, more deeply than any other English poet, the mysteries of nature.

On the face of it Wordsworth may seem to lack the qualities of a great writer. He had no sense of humour, which led him to write such appalling lines as, 'Spade with which Wilkinson hath tilled his lands'. As a general rule it's difficult to write seriously about life unless you can also be funny about it. He started off as a young romantic poet and liberal, an admirer of the French Revolution who went to France and fathered an illegitimate child by Marie Anne Vallon, the daughter of a Royalist family. He ended his life as an ageing reactionary, with his radical views forgotten. He lost the admiration of younger poets and Browning called him 'the Lost Leader' and wrote, 'Just for a handful of silver he left us.' None of these things have much relevance to his extraordinary perception of the natural world, and the greatness of his poetry at its best. Consider, for a moment, lines of such power and beauty that only Shakespeare, among other poets, might possibly have written:

> Knowing that nature never did betray
> The heart that loved her.

or

> Surprised by joy—impatient as the Wind
> I turned to share the transport—O! with whom
>   But Thee, deep buried in the silent tomb,
> That spot which no vicissitude can find?
> Love, faithful love, recall'd thee to my mind—
>   But how could I forget thee?

But the importance of Wordsworth is not in the poetry alone but in the effect he has on our attitude to the natural world. Those of us who cannot accept a personal God are yet discontented with mere materialism. We look perpetually for some magic in the passing moment, those sights and sounds which seem to have a significance beyond their physical existence, even if it is only the way in which they echo our need to believe in the power of the natural world. Wordsworth found his religion in the English landscape, and it has always seemed a very satisfactory sort of religion to me. Natural beauty was what he celebrated, what he recollected in moments of tranquility, and the basis of the creed expressed in the lines he wrote above Tintern Abbey:

>   For I have learned
> To look on nature, not as in the hour
> Of thoughtless youth; but hearing often times
> The still, sad music of humanity,
> Not harsh nor grating, though of ample power
> To chasten and subdue. And I have felt
> A presence that disturbs me with the joy
> Of elevated thoughts; a sense sublime
> Of something far more deeply interfused
> Whose dwelling is the light of setting suns,
> And the round ocean and the living air,
> And the blue sky, and in the mind of man:
> A motion and a spirit, that impels
> All thinking things, all objects of all thought,
> And rolls through all things.

A very different writer from Wordsworth, Charles Dickens, said that he dwelt purposefully on the romantic side of familiar things. Wordsworth has a similar effect; he comes, like all the best English poets, from the countryside, and finds in it not only great splendour but profound and religious feelings. What will happen to poetry and such feelings when England is covered with golf courses and motorways and theme parks doesn't bear thinking about. We will still have Wordsworth's poetry, beautifully illustrated here by Piers Browne, set in elegant type, and we can always remember the strange figure who paced the hills beneath his umbrella, and we can recollect his emotions in our own tranquility.

TURVILLE HEATH, 1991

WAS it for this
   That one, the fairest of all rivers, loved
To blend his murmurs with my nurse's song,
And, from his alder shades and rocky falls,
And from his fords and shallows, sent a voice
That flowed along my dreams? For this, didst thou,
O Derwent! winding among grassy holms
Where I was looking on, a babe in arms,
Make ceaseless music that composed my thoughts
To more than infant softness, giving me
Amid the fretful dwellings of mankind
A foretaste, a dim earnest, of the calm
That Nature breathes among the hills and groves.
When he had left the mountains and received
On his smooth breast the shadow of those towers
That yet survive, a shattered monument
Of feudal sway, the bright blue river passed
Along the margin of our terrace walk;
A tempting playmate whom we dearly loved.
Oh! many a time have I, a five years' child,
In a small mill-race severed from his stream,
Made one long bathing of a summer's day;
Basked in the sun, and plunged and basked again
Alternate, all a summer's day, or scoured
The sandy fields, leaping through flowery groves
Of yellow ragwort; or when rock and hill,
The woods, and distant Skiddaw's lofty height,
Were bronzed with deepest radiance, stood alone
Beneath the sky, as if I had been born

On Indian plains, and from my mother's hut
Had run abroad in wantonness, to sport
A naked savage, in the thunder shower.
    Fair seed-time had my soul, and I grew up
Fostered alike by beauty and by fear:
Much favoured in my birthplace, and no less

In that beloved Vale to which ere long
We were transplanted—there were we let loose
For sports of wider range. Ere I had told
Ten birth-days, when among the mountain-slopes
Frost, and the breath of frosty wind, had snapped
The last autumnal crocus, 'twas my joy
With store of springes o'er my shoulder hung
To range the open heights where woodcocks ran
Among the smooth green turf. Through half the night,

[2]

Scudding away from snare to snare, I plied
That anxious visitation;—moon and stars
Were shining o'er my head. I was alone,
And seemed to be a trouble to the peace
That dwelt among them. Sometimes it befell
In these night wanderings, that a strong desire
O'erpowered my better reason, and the bird
Which was the captive of another's toil
Became my prey; and when the deed was done
I heard among the solitary hills
Low breathings coming after me, and sounds
Of undistinguishable motion, steps
Almost as silent as the turf they trod.

NUTTING

IT seems a day
(I speak of one from many singled out)
One of those heavenly days that cannot die;
When, in the eagerness of boyish hope,
I left our cottage-threshold, sallying forth
With a huge wallet o'er my shoulders slung,
A nutting-crook in hand; and turned my steps
Tow'rd some far-distant wood, a Figure quaint,
Tricked out in proud disguise of cast-off weeds
Which for that service had been husbanded,
By exhortation of my frugal Dame—
Motley accoutrement, of power to smile
At thorns, and brakes, and brambles,—and in truth
More ragged than need was! O'er pathless rocks,
Through beds of matted fern, and tangled thickets,
Forcing my way, I came to one dear nook
Unvisited, where not a broken bough
Drooped with its withered leaves, ungracious sign
Of devastation; but the hazels rose
Tall and erect, with tempting clusters hung,
A virgin scene!—A little while I stood,
Breathing with such suppression of the heart
As joy delights in; and with wise restraint
Voluptuous, fearless of a rival, eyed
The banquet;—or beneath the trees I sate
Among the flowers, and with the flowers I played;
A temper known to those who, after long
And weary expectation, have been blest
With sudden happiness beyond all hope.

Perhaps it was a bower beneath whose leaves
The violets of five seasons re-appear
And fade, unseen by any human eye:
Where fairy water-breaks do murmur on
For ever; and I saw the sparkling foam,
And — with my cheek on one of those green stones
That, fleeced with moss, under the shady trees,
Lay round me, scattered like a flock of sheep —
I heard the murmur and the murmuring sound,
In that sweet mood when pleasure loves to pay
Tribute to ease; and, of its joy secure,
The heart luxuriates with indifferent things,
Wasting its kindliness on stocks and stones,
And on the vacant air. Then up I rose,
And dragged to earth both branch and bough, with crash
And merciless ravage: and the shady nook
Of hazels, and the green and mossy bower,
Deformed and sullied, patiently gave up
Their quiet being: and unless I now
Confound my present feelings with the past,
Ere from the mutilated bower I turned
Exulting, rich beyond the wealth of kings,
I felt a sense of pain when I beheld
The silent trees, and saw the intruding sky.
Then, dearest Maiden, move along these shades
In gentleness of heart; with gentle hand
Touch — for there is a spirit in the woods.

AND in the frosty season, when the sun
Was set, and visible for many a mile
The cottage windows through the twilight blazed,
I heeded not the summons: happy time
It was indeed for all of us — to me
It was a time of rapture! Clear and loud
The village clock tolled six, — I wheeled about,
Proud and exulting like an untired horse
That cares not for its home. All shod with steel,
We hissed along the polished ice in games
Confederate, imitative of the chase
And woodland pleasures, — the resounding horn,
The pack loud bellowing, and the hunted hare.
So through the darkness and the cold we flew,
And not a voice was idle; with the din,
Meanwhile, the precipices rang aloud;
The leafless trees and every icy crag
Tinkled like iron; while the distant hills
Into the tumult sent an alien sound
Of melancholy not unnoticed, while the stars
Eastward were sparkling clear, and in the west
The orange sky of evening died away.
Not seldom from the uproar I retired
Into a silent bay, or sportively
Glanced sideway, leaving the tumultuous throng,
To cut across the image of a star
That gleamed upon the ice; and oftentimes,
When we had given our bodies to the wind,
And all the shadowy banks on either side

Came sweeping through the darkness, spinning still
The rapid line of motion, then at once
Have I, reclining back upon my heels,
Stopped short; yet still the solitary cliffs
Wheeled by me — even as if the earth had rolled
With visible motion her diurnal round!
Behind me did they stretch in solemn train,
Feebler and feebler, and I stood and watched
Till all was tranquil as a dreamless sleep.

ONE Christmas-time,
The day before the holidays began,
Feverish, and tired, and restless, I went forth
Into the fields, impatient for the sight
Of those two horses which should bear us home;
My brothers and myself. There was a crag,
An eminence, which from the meeting-point
Of two highways ascending, overlooked
At least a long half-mile of those two roads,
By each of which the expected steeds might come,
The choice uncertain. Thither I repaired
Up to the highest summit; t'was a day
Stormy, and rough, and wild, and on the grass
I sate half-sheltered by a naked wall;
Upon my right hand was a single sheep,
A whistling hawthorn on my left, and there,
With those companions at my side, I watched,
Straining my eyes intensely, as the mist
Gave intermitting prospect of the wood
And plain beneath. Ere I to school returned
That dreary time, ere I had been ten days
A dweller in my father's house, he died,
And I and my two brothers, orphans then,
Followed his body to the grave. The event,
With all the sorrow which it brought, appeared
A chastisement; and when I called to mind
That day so lately passed, when from the crag
I looked in such anxiety of hope;
With trite reflections of morality,

Yet in the deepest passion, I bowed low
To God, Who thus corrected my desires;
And, afterwards, the wind and sleety rain,
And all the business of the elements,
The single sheep, and the one blasted tree,
And the bleak music of that old stone wall,
The noise of wood and water, and the mist
Which on the line of each of those two roads
Advanced in such indisputable shapes;
All these were spectacles and sounds to which
I often would repair, and thence would drink,
As at a fountain; and I do not doubt
That in this later time, when storm and rain
Beat on my roof at midnight, or by day,
When I am in the woods, unknown to me
The workings of my spirit thence are brought.

ONE summer evening (led by her) I found
A little boat tied to a willow tree
Within a rocky cave, it's usual home.
Straight I unloosed her chain, and stepping in
Pushed from the shore. It was an act of stealth
And troubled pleasure, nor without the voice
Of mountain-echoes did my boat move on;
Leaving behind her still, on either side,
Small circles glittering idly in the moon,
Until they melted all into one track
Of sparkling light. But now, like one who rows,
Proud of his skill, to reach a chosen point
With an unswerving line, I fixed my view
Upon the summit of a craggy ridge,
The horizon's utmost boundary, for above
Was nothing but the stars and the grey sky.
She was an elfin pinnace; lustily
I dipped my oars into the silent lake,
And, as I rose upon the stroke, my boat
Went heaving through the water like a swan;
When, from behind that craggy steep till then
The horizon's bound, a huge peak, black and huge,
As if with voluntary power instinct
Upreared its head. I struck and struck again,
And growing still in stature the grim shape
Towered up between me and the stars, and still,
For so it seemed, with purpose of its own
And measured motion like a living thing,
Strode after me. With trembling oars I turned,
And through the silent water stole my way
Back to the covert of the willow tree;
There in her mooring-place I left my bark,—
And through the meadows homeward went, in grave
And serious mood; but after I had seen

That spectacle, for many days, my brain
Worked with a dim and undetermined sense
Of unknown modes of being; o'er my thoughts
There hung a darkness, call it solitude
Or blank desertion. No familiar shapes
Remained, no pleasant images of trees,
Of sea or sky, no colours of green fields;
But huge and mighty forms, that do not live
Like living men, moved slowly through the mind
By day, and were a trouble to my dreams.

MID a throng
Of maids and youths, old men, and matrons staid,
A medley of all tempers, I had passed
The night in dancing, gaiety, and mirth,
With din of instruments and shuffling feet,
And glancing forms, and tapers glittering,
And unaimed prattle flying up and down;
Spirits upon the stretch, and here and there
Slight shocks of young love-liking interspersed,
Whose transient pleasure mounted to the head,
And tingled through the veins. Ere we retired,
The cock had crowed, and now the eastern sky
Was kindling, not unseen, from humble copse
And open field, through which the pathway wound,
And homeward led my steps. Magnificent
The morning rose, in memorable pomp,
Glorious as e'er I had beheld—in front,
The sea lay laughing at a distance; near,
The solid mountains shone, bright as the clouds,
Grain-tinctured, drenched in empyrean light;
And in the meadows and the lower grounds
Was all the sweetness of a common dawn—
Dews, vapours, and the melody of birds,
And labourers going forth to till the fields.

　　Ah! need I say, dear Friend! that to the brim
My heart was full; I made no vows, but vows
Were then made for me; bond unknown to me
Was given, that I should be, else sinning greatly,
A dedicated Spirit. On I walked
In thankful blessedness, which yet survives.

IT WAS a summer's night, a close warm night,
Wan, dull and glaring, with a dripping mist
Low-hung and thick that covered all the sky,
Half threatening storm and rain; but on we went
Unchecked, being full of heart and having faith
In our tried pilot. Little could we see
Hemmed round on every side with fog and damp,
And, after ordinary travellers' chat
With our conductor, silently we sank
Each into commerce with his private thoughts:
Thus did we breast the ascent, and by myself
Was nothing either seen or heard the while
Which took me from my musings, save that once
The shepherd's cur did to his own great joy
Unearth a hedgehog in the mountain crags
Round which he made a barking turbulent.
This small adventure, for even such it seemed
In that wild place and at the dead of night,
Being over and forgotten, on we wound
In silence as before. With forehead bent
Earthward, as if in opposition set
Against an enemy, I panted up
With eager pace, and no less eager thoughts.
Thus might we wear perhaps an hour away,
Ascending at loose distance each from each,
And I, as chanced, the foremost of the band;
When at my feet the ground appeared to brighten,
And with a step or two seemed brighter still;
Nor had I time to ask the cause of this,

For instantly a light upon the turf
Fell like a flash: I looked about, and lo!
The Moon stood naked in the heavens, at height
Immense above my head, and on the shore
I found myself of a huge sea of mist,
Which, meek and silent, rested at my feet.
A hundred hills their dusky backs upheaved
All over this still ocean; and beyond,
Far, far beyond, the vapours shot themselves,
In headlands, tongues, and promontory shapes,
Into the sea, the real sea, that seemed
To dwindle, and give up its majesty,
Usurped upon as far as sight could reach.
Meanwhile, the Moon looked down upon this show
In single glory, and we stood, the mist
Touching our very feet; and from the shore
At distance not the third part of a mile
Was a blue chasm; a fracture in the vapour,
A deep and gloomy breathing-space through which
Mounted the roar of waters, torrents, streams
Innumerable, roaring with one voice!
The universal spectacle throughout
Was shaped for admiration and delight,
Grand in itself alone, but in that breach
Through which the homeless voice of waters rose,
That dark deep thoroughfare, had Nature lodged
The soul, the imagination of the whole.

I TRAVELLED among unknown men,
In lands beyond the sea;
Nor, England! did I know till then
What love I bore to thee.

'Tis past, that melancholy dream!
Nor will I quit thy shore
A second time; for still I seem
To love thee more and more.

Among thy mountains did I feel
The joy of my desire;
And she I cherished turned her wheel
Beside an English fire.

Thy mornings showed, thy nights concealed,
The bowers where Lucy played;
And thine too is the last green field
That Lucy's eye surveyed.

[18]

LINES COMPOSED A FEW MILES ABOVE
TINTERN ABBEY

on revisiting the banks of the Wye during a tour, 13 July 1798

FIVE years have past; five summers, with the length
Of five long winters! and again I hear
These waters, rolling from their mountain-springs
With a soft inland murmur.—Once again
Do I behold these steep and lofty cliffs,
That on a wild secluded scene impress
Thoughts of more deep seclusion; and connect
The landscape with the quiet of the sky.
The day is come when I again repose
Here, under this dark sycamore, and view
These plots of cottage-ground, these orchard-tufts,
Which at this season, with their unripe fruits,
Are clad in one green hue, and lose themselves
'Mid groves and copses. Once again I see
These hedge-rows, hardly hedge-rows, little lines
Of sportive wood run wild: these pastoral farms,
Green to the very door; and wreaths of smoke
Sent up in silence, from among the trees!
With some uncertain notice, as might seem
Of vagrant dwellers in the houseless woods,
Or of some Hermit's cave, where by his fire
The Hermit sits alone.
                        These beauteous forms,
Through a long absence, have not been to me
As is a landscape to a blind man's eye:
But oft, in lonely rooms, and 'mid the din
Of towns and cities, I have owed to them,

In hours of weariness, sensations sweet,
Felt in the blood, and felt along the heart;
And passing even into my purer mind,
With tranquil restoration:—feelings too
Of unremembered pleasure: such, perhaps,
As have no slight or trivial influence
On that best portion of a good man's life,
His little, nameless, unremembered, acts
Of kindness and of love. Nor less, I trust,
To them I may have owed another gift,
Of aspect more sublime; that blessed mood,
In which the burthen of the mystery,
In which the heavy and the weary weight
Of all this unintelligible world,
Is lightened:—that serene and blessed mood,
In which the affections gently lead us on,—

Until, the breath of this corporeal frame
And even the motion of our human blood
Almost suspended, we are laid asleep
In body, and become a living soul:
While with an eye made quiet by the power
Of harmony, and the deep power of joy,
We see into the life of things.
                                    If this
Be but a vain belief, yet, oh! how oft—
In darkness and amid the many shapes
Of joyless daylight; when the fretful stir
Unprofitable, and the fever of the world,
Have hung upon the beatings of my heart—
How oft, in spirit, have I turned to thee,
O sylvan Wye! thou wanderer thro' the woods,
How often has my spirit turned to thee!
    And now, with gleams of half-extinguished thought,
With many recognitions dim and faint,
And somewhat of a sad perplexity,
The picture of the mind revives again:
While here I stand, not only with the sense
Of present pleasure, but with pleasing thoughts
That in this moment there is life and food
For future years. And so I dare to hope,
Though changed, no doubt, from what I was when first
I came among these hills; when like a roe
I bounded o'er the mountains, by the sides
Of the deep rivers, and the lonely streams,
Wherever nature led: more like a man
Flying from something that he dreads than one
Who sought the thing he loved. For nature then
(The coarser pleasures of my boyish days,
And their glad animal movements all gone by)
To me was all in all.—I cannot paint

What then I was. The sounding cataract
Haunted me like a passion: the tall rock,
The mountain, and the deep and gloomy wood,
Their colours and their forms, were then to me
An appetite; a feeling and a love,
That had no need of a remoter charm,
By thought supplied, nor any interest
Unborrowed from the eye.—That time is past,
And all its aching joys are now no more,
And all its dizzy raptures. Not for this
Faint I, nor mourn nor murmur; other gifts
Have followed; for such loss, I would believe,
Abundant recompense. For I have learned
To look on nature, not as in the hour
Of thoughtless youth; but hearing oftentimes
The still, sad music of humanity,
Nor harsh nor grating, though of ample power
To chasten and subdue. And I have felt
A presence that disturbs me with the joy
Of elevated thoughts; a sense sublime
Of something far more deeply interfused,
Whose dwelling is the light of setting suns,
And the round ocean and the living air,
And the blue sky, and in the mind of man:
A motion and a spirit, that impels
All thinking things, all objects of all thought,
And rolls through all things. Therefore am I still
A lover of the meadows and the woods,
And mountains; and of all that we behold
From this green earth; of all the mighty world
Of eye, and ear,—both what they half create,
And what perceive; well pleased to recognise
In nature and the language of the sense
The anchor of my purest thoughts, the nurse,

The guide, the guardian of my heart, and soul
Of all my moral being.
                    Nor perchance,
If I were not thus taught, should I the more
Suffer my genial spirits to decay:
For thou art with me here upon the banks
Of this fair river; thou my dearest Friend,
My dear, dear Friend; and in thy voice I catch
The language of my former heart, and read
My former pleasures in the shooting lights
Of thy wild eyes. Oh! yet a little while
May I behold in thee what I was once,
My dear, dear Sister! and this prayer I make,
Knowing that Nature never did betray
The heart that loved her; 'tis her privilege,
Through all the years of this our life, to lead
From joy to joy: for she can so inform
The mind that is within us, so impress
With quietness and beauty, and so feed
With lofty thoughts, that neither evil tongues,
Rash judgements, nor the sneers of selfish men,
Nor greetings where no kindness is, nor all
The dreary intercourse of daily life,
Shall e'er prevail against us, or disturb
Our cheerful faith, that all which we behold
Is full of blessings. Therefore let the moon
Shine on thee in thy solitary walk;
And let the misty mountain-winds be free
To blow against thee: and, in after years,
When these wild ecstasies shall be matured
Into a sober pleasure; when thy mind
Shall be a mansion for all lovely forms,
Thy memory be as a dwelling-place
For all sweet sounds and harmonies; oh! then,

If solitude, or fear, or pain, or grief,
Should be thy portion, with what healing thoughts
Of tender joy wilt though remember me,
And these my exhortations! Nor, perchance—
If I should be where I no more can hear
Thy voice, nor catch from thy wild eyes these gleams
Of past existence—wilt thou then forget
That on the banks of this delightful stream
We stood together; and that I, so long
A worshipper of Nature, hither came
Unwearied in that service: rather say
With warmer love—oh! with far deeper zeal
Of holier love. Nor wilt thou then forget
That after many wanderings, many years
Of absence, these steep woods and lofty cliffs,
And this green pastoral landscape, were to me
More dear, both for themselves and for thy sake!

ANIMAL TRANQUILLITY AND DECAY

THE little hedgerow birds,
   That peck along the road, regard him not.
He travels on, and in his face, his step,
His gait, is one expression: every limb,
His look and bending figure, all bespeak
A man who does not move with pain, but moves
With thought.—He is insensibly subdued
To settled quiet: he is one by whom
All effort seems forgotten; one to whom
Long patience hath such mild composure given,
That patience now doth seem a thing of which
He hath no need. He is by nature led
To peace so perfect that the young behold
With envy, what the Old Man hardly feels.

A SLUMBER did my spirit seal;
   I had no human fears:
She seemed a thing that could not feel
   The touch of earthly years.

No motion has she now, no force;
   She neither hears nor sees;
Rolled round in earth's diurnal course,
   With rocks, and stones, and trees.

SHE dwelt among the untrodden ways
    Beside the springs of Dove,
A Maid whom there were none to praise
    And very few to love:

A violet by a mossy stone
    Half hidden from the eye!
—Fair as a star, when only one
    Is shining in the sky.

She lived unknown, and few could know
    When Lucy ceased to be;
But she is in her grave, and, oh,
    The difference to me!

A COMPLAINT

THERE is a change—and I am poor;
Your love hath been, nor long ago,
A fountain at my fond heart's door,
Whose only business was to flow;
And flow it did; not taking heed
Of its own bounty, or my need.

What happy moments did I count!
Blest was I then all bliss above!
Now, for that consecrated fount
Of murmuring, sparkling, living love,
What have I? shall I dare to tell?
A comfortless and hidden well.

A well of love—it may be deep—
I trust it is,—and never dry:
What matter? if the waters sleep
In silence and obscurity.
—Such change, and at the very door
Of my fond heart, hath made me poor.

I WANDERED lonely as a cloud
That floats on high o'er vales and hills,
When all at once I saw a crowd,
A host, of golden daffodils;
Beside the lake, beneath the trees,
Fluttering and dancing in the breeze.

Continuous as the stars that shine
And twinkle on the milky way,
They stretched in never-ending line
Along the margin of a bay:
Ten thousand saw I at a glance,
Tossing their heads in sprightly dance.

The waves beside them danced; but they
Out-did the sparkling waves in glee:
A poet could not but be gay,
In such a jocund company:
I gazed—and gazed—but little thought
What wealth the show to me had brought:

For oft, when on my couch I lie
In vacant or in pensive mood,
They flash upon that inward eye
Which is the bliss of solitude;
And then my heart with pleasure fills,
And dances with the daffodils.

SONNET

BROOK! whose society the Poet seeks,
Intent his wasted spirits to renew;
And whom the curious Painter doth pursue
Through rocky passes, among flowery creeks,
And tracks thee dancing down thy waterbreaks;
If wish were mine some type of thee to view,
Thee, and not thee thyself, I would not do
Like Grecian Artists, give thee human cheeks,
Channels for tears; no Naiad shouldst thou be,—
Have neither limbs, feet, feathers, joints, nor hairs:
It seems the Eternal Soul is clothed in thee
With purer robes than those of flesh and blood,
And hath bestowed on thee a safer good;
Unwearied joy, and life without its cares.

[30]

SONNET: TO SLEEP

A FLOCK of sheep that leisurely pass by,
One after one; the sound of rain, and bees
Murmuring; the fall of rivers, winds and seas,
Smooth fields, white sheets of water, and pure sky;
I have thought of all by turns, and yet do lie
Sleepless! and soon the small birds' melodies
Must hear, first uttered from my orchard trees;
And the first cuckoo's melancholy cry.
Even thus last night, and two nights more, I lay
And could not win thee, Sleep! by any stealth:
So do not let me wear to-night away:
Without Thee what is all the morning's wealth?
Come, blessed barrier between day and day,
Dear mother of fresh thoughts and joyous health!

THE world is too much with us; late and soon,
  Getting and spending, we lay waste our powers:
Little we see in Nature that is ours;
We have given our hearts away, a sordid boon!
This Sea that bares her bosom to the moon;
The winds that will be howling at all hours,
And are up-gathered now like sleeping flowers;
For this, for everything, we are out of tune;
It moves us not.—Great God! I'd rather be
A Pagan suckled in a creed outworn;
So might I, standing on this pleasant lea,
Have glimpses that would make me less forlorn;
Have sight of Proteus rising from the sea;
Or hear old Triton blow his wreathed horn.

[32]

THE WHITE DOE OF RYLSTONE

FROM Bolton's old monastic tower
The bells ring loud with gladsome power;
The sun shines bright; the fields are gay
With people in their best array
Of stole and doublet, hood and scarf,
Along the banks of crystal Wharf,
Through the Vale retired and lowly,
Trooping to that summons holy.
And, up among the moorlands, see
What sprinklings of blithe company!
Of lasses and of shepherd grooms,
That down the steep hills force their way,
Like cattle through the budded brooms;
Path, or no path, what care they?
And thus in joyous mood they hie
To Bolton's mouldering Priory.

What would they there?—full fifty years
That sumptuous Pile, with all its peers,
Too harshly hath been doomed to taste
The bitterness of wrong and waste:
Its courts are ravaged; but the tower
Is standing with a voice of power,
That ancient voice which wont to call
To mass or some high festival;
And in the shattered fabric's heart
Remaineth one protected part;
A Chapel, like a wild-bird's nest,
Closely embowered and trimly drest;
And thither young and old repair,
This Sabbath-day, for praise and prayer.

Fast the churchyard fills;—anon
Look again, and they are all gone;
The cluster round the porch, and the folk
Who sate in the shade of the Prior's Oak!
And scarecly have they disappeared
Ere the prelusive hymn is heard:—
With one consent the people rejoice,
Filling the church with a lofty voice!

SONNET

SURPRISED by joy—impatient as the Wind
I turned to share the transport—Oh! with whom
But Thee, deep buried in the silent tomb,
That spot which no vicissitude can find?
Love, faithful love, recalled thee to my mind—
But how could I forget thee? Through what power,
Even for the least division of an hour,
Have I been so beguiled as to be blind
To my most grievous loss!—That thought's return
Was the worst pang that sorrow ever bore,
Save one, one only, when I stood forlorn,
Knowing my heart's best treasure was no more;
That neither present time, nor years unborn
Could to my sight that heavenly face restore.

A WREN'S NEST

AMONG the dwellings framed by birds
In field or forest with nice care,
Is none that with the little Wren's
    In snugness may compare.

No door the tenement requires,
    And seldom needs a laboured roof;
Yet is it to the fiercest sun
    Impervious, and storm-proof.

[36]

So warm, so beautiful withal,
    In perfect fitness for its aim,
That to the Kind by special grace
    Their instinct surely came.

And when for their abodes they seek
    An opportune recess,
The hermit has no finer eye
    For shadowy quietness.

These find, 'mid ivied abbey-walls,
    A canopy in some still nook;
Others are pent-housed by a brae
    That overhangs a brook.

There to the brooding bird her mate
    Warbles by fits his low clear song;
And by the busy streamlet both
    Are sung to all day long.

Or in sequestered lanes they build,
    Where, till the flitting bird's return,
Her eggs within the nest repose,
    Like relics in an urn.

But still, where general choice is good,
    There is a better and a best;
And, among fairest objects, some
    Are fairer than the rest;

This, one of those small builders proved
    In a green covert, where, from out
The forehead of a pollard oak,
    The leafy antlers sprout;

For She who planned the mossy lodge,
    Mistrusting her evasive skill,
Had to a Primrose looked for aid
    Her wishes to fulfil.

High on the trunk's projecting brow,
    And fixed an infant's span above
The budding flowers, peeped forth the nest
    The prettiest of the grove!

The treasure proudly did I show
    To some whose minds without disdain
Can turn to little things; but once
    Looked up for it in vain:

'Tis gone—a ruthless spoiler's prey,
    Who heeds not beauty, love, or song,
'Tis gone! (so seemed it) and we grieved
    Indignant at the wrong.

Just three days after, passing by
    In clearer light the moss-built cell
I saw, espied its shaded mouth;
    And felt that all was well.

The Primrose for a veil had spread
    The largest of her upright leaves;
And thus, for purposes benign,
    A simple flower deceives.

Concealed from friends who might disturb
    Thy quiet with no ill intent,
Secure from evil eyes and hands
    On barbarous plunder bent,

Rest, Mother-bird! and when thy young
　　Take flight, and thou art free to roam,
When withered is the guardian Flower,
　　And empty thy late home,

Think how ye prospered, thou and thine,
　　Amid the unviolated grove
Housed near the growing Primrose-tuft
　　In foresight, or in love.

SEPTEMBER 1815

WHILE not a leaf seems faded; while the fields,
With ripening harvest prodigally fair,
In brightest sunshine bask; this nipping air,
Sent from some distant clime where Winter wields
His icy scimitar, a foretaste yields
Of bitter change, and bids the flowers beware;
And whispers to the silent birds, 'Prepare
Against the threatening foe your trustiest shields.'
For me, who under kindlier laws belong
To Nature's tuneful quire, this rustling dry
Through leaves yet green, and yon crystalline sky,
Announce a season potent to renew,
'Mid frost and snow, the instinctive joys of song,
And nobler cares than listless summer knew.

AT FURNESS ABBEY

WELL have yon Railway Labourers to *this* ground
Withdrawn for noontide rest. They sit, they walk
Among the Ruins, but no idle talk
Is heard; to grave demeanour all are bound;
And from one voice a Hymn with tuneful sound
Hallows once more the long-deserted Quire
And thrills the old sepulchral earth, around.
Others look up, and with fixed eyes admire
That wide-spanned arch, wondering how it was raised,
To keep, so high in air, its strength and grace:
All seem to feel the spirit of the place,
And by the general reverance God is praised:
Profane Despoilers, stand ye not reproved,
While thus these simple-hearted men are moved?

ODE

INTIMATIONS OF IMMORTALITY FROM RECOLLECTIONS OF EARLY CHILDHOOD

The Child is father of the Man;
And I could wish my days to be
Bound each to each by natural piety.

THERE was a time when meadow, grove, and stream,
The earth, and every common sight,
        To me did seem
        Apparelled in celestial light,
The glory and the freshness of a dream.
It is not now as it hath been of yore;—
        Turn wheresoe'er I may,
            By night or day,
The things which I have seen I now can see no more.

II   The Rainbow comes and goes,
            And lovely is the Rose,
            The Moon doth with delight
        Look round her when the heavens are bare,
            Waters on a starry night
            Are beautiful and fair;
        The sunshine is a glorious birth;
        But yet I know, where'er I go,
That there hath past away a glory from the earth.

III   Now, while the birds thus sing a joyous song,
            And while the young lambs bound

[44]

As to the tabor's sound,
To me alone there came a thought of grief:
A timely utterance gave that thought relief,
        And I again am strong:
The cataracts blow their trumpets from the steep;
No more shall grief of mine the season wrong;
I hear the Echoes through the mountains throng,
The Winds come to me from the fields of sleep,
        And all the earth is gay;
                Land and sea
        Give themselves up to jollity,
            And with the heart of May
        Doth every Beast keep holiday;—
            Thou Child of Joy,
Shout round me, let me hear thy shouts, thou happy Shepherd-boy!

IV   Ye blessed Creatures, I have heard the call
        Ye to each other make; I see
The heavens laugh with you in your jubilee;
        My heart is at your festival,
            My head hath its coronal,
The fulness of your bliss, I feel—I feel it all.
            Oh evil day! if I were sullen
            While Earth herself is adorning,
                This sweet May-morning,
            And the Children are culling
                On every side,
            In a thousand valleys far and wide,
            Fresh flowers; while the sun shines warm,
And the Babe leaps up on his Mother's arm:—
            I hear, I hear, with joy I hear!
            —But there's a Tree, of many, one,
A single Field which I have looked upon,
Both of them speak of something that is gone:

The Pansy at my feet
    Doth the same tale repeat:
Whither is fled the visionary gleam?
Where is it now, the glory and the dream?

V   Our birth is but a sleep and a forgetting:
The Soul that rises with us, our life's Star,
        Hath had elsewhere its setting,
            And cometh from afar:
        Not in entire forgetfulness,
        And not in utter nakedness,
But trailing clouds of glory do we come
        From God, who is our home:
Heaven lies about us in our infancy!
Shades of the prison-house begin to close
        Upon the growing Boy
But He beholds the light, and whence it flows,
        He sees it in his joy;
The Youth, who daily farther from the east
        Must travel, still is Nature's Priest,
        And by the vision splendid
        Is on his way attended;
At length the Man perceives it die away,
And fade into the light of common day.

VI Earth fills her lap with pleasures of her own;
Yearnings she hath in her own natural kind,
And, even with something of a Mother's mind,
        And no unworthy aim,
        The homely Nurse doth all she can
To make her Foster-child, her Inmate Man,
        Forget the glories he hath known,
And that imperial palace whence he came.

VII   Behold the Child among his new-born blisses,
A six years' Darling of a pigmy size!
See, where 'mid work of his own hand he lies,
Fretted by sallies of his mother's kisses,
With light upon him from his father's eyes!
See, at his feet, some little plan or chart,
Some fragment from his dream of human life,
Shaped by himself with newly-learned art;
      A wedding or a festival,
      A mourning or a funeral;
        And this hath now his heart,
      And unto this he frames his song:

[48]

                  Then will he fit his tongue
To dialogues of business, love, or strife;
            But it will not be long
            Ere this be thrown aside,
            And with new joy and pride
The little Actor cons another part;
Filling from time to time his 'humorous stage'
With all the Persons, down to palsied Age,
That Life brings with her in her equipage;
            As if his whole vocation
            Were endless imitation.

VIII Thou, whose exterior semblance doth belie
            Thy Soul's immensity;
Thou best Philosopher, who yet dost keep
Thy heritage, thou Eye among the blind,
That, deaf and silent, read'st the eternal deep,
Haunted for ever by the eternal mind,—
            Mighty Prophet! Seer blest!
            On whom those truths do rest,
Which we are toiling all our lives to find,
In darkness lost, the darkness of the grave;
Thou, over whom thy Immortality
Broods like the Day, a Master o'er a Slave,
A Presence which is not to be put by;
            [To whom the grave
Is but a lonely bed without the sense or sight
            Of day or the warm light,
A place of thought where we in waiting lie;]
Thou little Child, yet glorious in the might
Of heaven-born freedom on thy being's height,
Why with such earnest pains dost thou provoke
The years to bring the inevitable yoke,
Thus blindly with thy blessedness at strife?

Full soon thy Soul shall have her earthly freight,
And custom lie upon thee with a weight,
Heavy as frost, and deep almost as life!

IX   O joy! that in our embers
        Is something that doth live,
        That nature yet remembers
        What was so fugitive!
The thought of our past years in me doth breed
Perpetual benediction: not indeed
For that which is most worthy to be blest;
Delight and liberty, the simple creed
Of Childhood, whether busy or at rest,
With new-fledged hope still fluttering in his breast:—
        Not for these I raise
        The song of thanks and praise;
     But for those obstinate questionings
     Of sense and outward things,
     Fallings from us, vanishings;
     Blank misgivings of a Creature
Moving about in worlds not realised,
High instincts before which our mortal Nature
Did tremble like a guilty Thing surprised:
        But for those first affections,
        Those shadowy recollections,
     Which, be they what they may,
Are yet the fountain-light of all our day,
Are yet a master-light of all our seeing;
     Uphold us, cherish, and have power to make
Our noisy years seem moments in the being
Of the eternal Silence: truths that wake,
        To perish never:
Which neither listlessness, nor mad endeavour,
        Nor man nor Boy,

[50]

Nor all that is at enmity with joy,
Can utterly abolish or destroy!
　　Hence in a season of calm weather
　　　Though inland far we be,
Our Souls have sight of that immortal sea
　　　Which brought us hither,
　　Can in a moment travel thither,
And see the Children sport upon the shore,
And hear the mighty waters rolling evermore.

x　Then sing, ye Birds, sing, sing a joyous song!
　　　And let the young Lambs bound
　　　As to the tabor's sound!
We in thought will join your throng,
　　　Ye that pipe and ye that play,
　　　Ye that through your hearts today
　　　Feel the gladness of the May!
What though the radiance which was once so bright
Be now forever taken from my sight,
　　Though nothing can bring back the hour
Of splendour in the grass, of glory in the flower;
　　　We will grieve not, rather find
　　　Strength in what remains behind;
　　　In the primal sympathy
　　　Which having been must ever be;
　　　In the soothing thoughts that spring
　　　Out of human suffering;
　　　In the faith that looks through death,
In years that bring the philosophic mind.

XI　And O, ye Fountains, Meadows, Hills and Groves,
Forebode not any severing of your loves!
Yet in my heart of hearts I feel your might;
I only have relinquished one delight

To live beneath your more habitual sway.
I love the Brooks which down their channels fret,
Even more than when I tripped lightly as they;
The innocent brightness of a new-born Day
      Is lovely yet;
The Clouds that gather round the setting sun
Do take a sober colouring from an eye
That hath kept watch o'er man's mortality;
Another race hath been, and other palms are won.
Thanks to the human heart by which we live,
Thanks to its tenderness, its joys, and fears,
To me the meanest flower that blows can give
Thoughts that do often lie too deep for tears.

TO MY SISTER

IT is the first mild day of March:
Each minute sweeter than before,
The redbreast sings from the tall larch
That stands beside our door.

There is a blessing in the air,
Which seems a sense of joy to yield
To the bare trees, and mountains bare,
And grass in the green field.

My sister! ('tis a wish of mine)
Now that our morning meal is done,
Make haste, your morning task resign;
Come forth and feel the sun.

Edward will come with you;—and, pray,
Put on with speed your woodland dress;
And bring no book: for this one day
We'll give to idleness.

No joyless forms shall regulate
Our living calendar:
We from to-day, my Friend, will date
The opening of the year.

Love, now a universal birth,
From heart to heart is stealing,
From earth to man, from man to earth:
—It is the hour of feeling.

One moment now may give us more
Than years of toiling reason:
Our minds shall drink at every pore
The spirit of the season.

Some silent laws our hearts will make,
Which they shall long obey:
We for the year to come may take
Our temper from to-day.

And from the blessed power that rolls
About, below, above,
We'll frame the measure of our souls:
They shall be tuned to love.

Then come, my Sister! come, I pray,
With speed put on your woodland dress;
And bring no book: for this one day
We'll give to idleness.

NOVEMBER I

HOW clear, how keen, how marvellously bright
The effluence from yon distant mountain's head,
Which, strewn with snow smooth as the sky can shed,
Shines like another sun—on mortal sight
Uprisen, as if to check approaching Night,
And all her twinkling stars. Who now would tread,
If so he might, yon mountain's glittering head—
Terrestrial, but a surface, by the flight
Of sad mortality's earth-sullying wing,
Unswept, unstained? Nor shall the aerial Powers
Dissolve that beauty, destined to endure,
White, radiant, spotless, exquisitely pure,
Through all vicissitudes, till genial Spring
Has filled the laughing vales with welcome flowers.

GORDALE

AT early dawn, or rather when the air
Glimmers with fading light, and shadowy Eve
Is busiest to confer and to bereave;
Then, pensive Votary! let thy feet repair
To Gordale-chasm, terrific as the lair
Where the young lions couch; for so, by leave
Of the propitious hour, thou may'st perceive
The local Deity, with oozy hair
And mineral crown, beside his jagged urn,
Recumbent: Him thou may'st behold, who hides
His lineaments by day, yet there presides,
Teaching the docile waters how to turn,
Or (if need be) impediment to spurn,
And force their passage to the salt-sea tides!

EVEN so for me a Vision sanctified
The sway of Death; long ere mine eyes had seen
Thy countenance—the still rapture of thy mien—
When thou, dear Sister! wert become Death's Bride:
No trace of pain or languor could abide
That change:—age on thy brow was smoothed—thy cold
Wan cheek at once privileged to unfold
A loveliness to living youth denied.
Oh! if within me hope should e'er decline,
The lamp of faith, lost Friend! too faintly burn;
Then may that heaven-revealing smile of thine,
The bright assurance, visibly return:
And let my spirit in that power divine
Rejoice, as, through that power, it ceased to mourn.

STRANGE fits of passion have I known:
And I will dare to tell,
But in the Lover's ear alone,
What once to me befell.

When she I loved looked every day
Fresh as a rose in June,
I to her cottage bent my way,
Beneath an evening-moon.

Upon the moon I fixed my eye,
All over the wide lea;
With quickening pace my horse drew nigh
Those paths so dear to me.

And now we reached the orchard-plot;
And, as we climbed the hill,
The sinking moon to Lucy's cot
Came near, and nearer still.

In one of those sweet dreams I slept,
Kind Nature's gentlest boon!
And all the while my eyes I kept
On the descending moon.

My horse moved on; hoof after hoof
He raised, and never stopped:
When down behind the cottage roof,
At once, the bright moon dropped.

What fond and wayward thoughts will slide
 Into a Lover's head!
'O mercy!' to myself I cried,
'If Lucy should be dead!'

THERE WAS A BOY

THERE was a Boy; ye knew him well, ye cliffs
And islands of Winander!—many a time,
At evening, when the earliest stars began
To move along the edges of the hills,
Rising or setting, would he stand alone,
Beneath the trees, or by the glimmering lake;
And there, with fingers interwoven, both hands
Pressed closely palm to palm and to his mouth
Uplifted, he, as through an instrument,
Blew mimic hootings to the silent owls,
That they might answer him.—And they would shout
Across the watery vale, and shout again,
Responsive to his call,—with quivering peals,
And long halloos, and screams, and echoes loud
Redoubled and redoubled; concourse wild
Of jocund din! And, when there came a pause
Of silence such as baffled his best skill:
Then sometimes, in that silence, while he hung
Listening, a gentle shock of mild surprise
Has carried far into his heart the voice
Of mountain-torrents; or the visible scene
Would enter unawares into his mind
With all its solemn imagery, its rocks,
Its woods, and that uncertain heaven received
Into the bosom of the steady lake.

   This boy was taken from his mates, and died
In childhood, ere he was full twelve years old.
Pre-eminent in beauty is the vale

Where he was born and bred: the churchyard hangs
Upon a slope above the village-school;
And through that churchyard when my way has led
On summer-evenings, I believe that there
A long half-hour together I have stood
Mute—looking at the grave in which he lies!

LONDON, 1802

MILTON! thou shouldst be living at this hour:
England hath need of thee: she is a fen
Of stagnant waters: altar, sword, and pen,
Fireside, the heroic wealth of hall and bower,
Have forfeited their ancient English dower
Of inward happiness. We are selfish men;
Oh! raise us up, return to us again;
And give us manners, virtue, freedom, power.
Thy soul was like a Star, and dwelt apart;
Thou hadst a voice whose sound was like the sea:
Pure as the naked heavens, majestic, free.
So didst thou travel on life's common way,
In cheerful godliness; and yet thy heart
The lowliest duties on herself did lay.

COMPOSED BY THE SIDE OF GRASMERE LAKE

CLOUDS, lingering yet, extend in solid bars
Through the grey west; and lo! these waters, steeled
By breezeless air to smoothest polish, yield
A vivid repetition of the stars;
Jove, Venus, and the ruddy crest of Mars
Amid his fellows beauteously revealed
At happy distance from earth's groaning field,
Where ruthless mortals wage incessant wars.
Is it a mirror?—or the nether Sphere
Opening to view the abyss in which she feeds
Her own calm fires?—But list! a voice is near;
Great Pan himself low-whispering through the reeds,
'Be thankful, thou; for if unholy deeds
Ravage the world, tranquillity is here!'

ON Man, on Nature, and on Human Life,
Musing in solitude, I oft perceive
Fair trains of imagery before me rise,
Accompanied by feelings of delight
Pure, or with no unpleasing sadness mixed,
And I am conscious of affecting thoughts
And dear remembrances, whose presence soothes
Or elevates the Mind, intent to weigh
The good and evil of our mortal state.
—To these emotions, whencesoe'er they come,
Whether from breath of outward circumstance,
Or from the Soul—an impulse to herself—
I would give utterance in numerous verse.
Of Truth, of Grandeur, Beauty, Love, and Hope,
And melancholy Fear subdued by Faith;
Of blessed consolations in distress;
Of moral strength, and intellectual Power;
Of joy in widest commonalty spread;
Of the individual Mind that keeps her own
Inviolate retirement, subject there
To Conscience only, and the law supreme
Of that Intelligence which governs all—
I sing:—'fit audience let me find though few!'

    So prayed, more gaining than he asked, the Bard—
In holiest mood. Urania, I shall need
Thy guidance, or a greater Muse, if such
Descend to earth or dwell in highest heaven!
For I must tread on shadowy ground, must sink

Deep—and, aloft ascending, breathe in worlds
To which the heaven of heavens is but a veil.
All strength—all terror, single or in bands,
That ever was put forth in personal form—
Jehovah—with his thunder, and the choir
Of shouting Angels, and the empyreal thrones—
I pass them unalarmed. Not Chaos, not
The darkest pit of lowest Erebus,
Nor aught of blinder vacancy, scooped out
By help of dreams—can breed such fear and awe
As fall upon us often when we look
Into our Minds, into the Mind of Man—
My haunt, and the main region of my song.
—Beauty—a living Presence of the earth,
Surpassing the most fair ideal Forms
Which craft of delicate Spirits hath composed
From earth's materials—waits upon my steps;
Pitches her tents before me as I move,
An hourly neighbour. Paradise, and groves
Elysian, Fortunate Fields—like those of old
Sought in the Atlantic Main—why should they be
A history only of departed things,
Or a mere fiction of what never was?
For the discerning intellect of Man,
When wedded to this goodly universe
In love and holy passion, shall find these
A simple produce of the common day.
—I, long before the blissful hour arrives,
Would chant, in lonely peace, the spousal verse
Of this great consummation:—and, by words
Which speak of nothing more than what we are,
Would I arouse the sensual from their sleep
Of Death, and win the vacant and the vain
To noble raptures; while my voice proclaims

[66]

How exquisitely the individual Mind
(And the progressive powers perhaps no less
Of the whole species) to the external World
Is fitted:—and how exquisitely, too—
Theme this but little heard of among men—
The external World is fitted to the Mind;
And the creation (by no lower name
Can it be called) which they with blended might
Accomplish:—this is our high argument.
—Such grateful haunts foregoing, if I oft
Must turn elsewhere—to travel near the tribes
And fellowships of men, and see ill sights
Of madding passions mutually inflamed;
Must hear Humanity in fields and groves
Pipe solitary anguish; or must hang
Brooding above the fierce confederate storm
Of sorrow, barricadoed evermore
Within the walls of cities—may these sounds
Have their authentic comment; that even these
Hearing, I be not downcast or forlorn!—
Descend, prophetic Spirit! that inspir'st
The human Soul of universal earth,
Dreaming on things to come; and dost possess
A metropolitan temple in the hearts
Of mighty Poets: upon me bestow
A gift of genuine insight; that my Song
With star-like virtue in its place may shine,
Shedding benignant influence, and secure,
Itself, from all malevolent effect
Of those mutations that extend their sway
Throughout the nether sphere!—And if with this
I mix more lowly matter; with the thing
Contemplated, describe the Mind and Man
Contemplating; and who, and what he was—

The transitory Being that beheld
This Vision; when and where, and how he lived;—
Be not this labour useless. If such theme
May sort with highest objects, then—dread Power!
Whose gracious favour is the primal source
Of all illumination,—may my Life
Express the image of a better time,
More wise desires, and simpler manners;—nurse
My Heart in genuine freedom:—all pure thoughts
Be with me;—so shall thy unfailing love
Guide, and support, and cheer me to the end!

TO A SKYLARK

ETHEREAL minstrel! pilgrim of the sky!
Dost thou despise the earth where cares abound?
Or, while the wings aspire, are heart and eye
Both with thy nest upon the dewy ground?
Thy nest which thou canst drop into at will,
Those quivering wings composed, that music still!

Leave to the nightingale her shady wood;
A privacy of glorious light is thine;
Whence thou dost pour upon the world a flood
Of harmony, with instinct more divine;
Type of the wise who soar, but never roam;
True to the kindred points of Heaven and Home!

O FRIEND! few happier moments have been mine
Through my whole life than that when first I heard
That this foul Tribe of Moloch was o'erthrown,
And their chief regent levelled with the dust.
The day was one which haply may deserve
A separate chronicle. Having gone abroad
From a small village where I tarried then,
To the same far-secluded privacy
I was returning. Over the smooth sands
Of Leven's ample estuary lay
My journey, and beneath a genial sun,
With distant prospect among gleams of sky
And clouds, and intermingled mountain tops,
In one inseparable glory clad,
Creatures of one ethereal substance met
In consistory, like a diadem
Or crown of burning seraphs as they sit
In the empyrean. Underneath this show
Lay, as I knew, the nest of pastoral vales
Among whose happy fields I had grown up
From childhood. On the fulgent spectacle,
Which neither changed nor stirred nor passed away,
I gazed, and with a fancy more alive
On this account, that I had chanced to find
That morning, ranging through the churchyard graves
Of Cartmel's rural town, the place in which
An honoured teacher of my youth was laid.
While we were schoolboys he had died among us,
And was borne hither, as I knew, to rest

With his own family. A plain stone, inscribed
With name, date, office, pointed out the spot,
To which a slip of verses was subjoined,
(By his desire, as afterwards I learnt)
A fragment from the elegy of Gray.
A week, or little less, before his death
He had said to me, 'My head will soon lie low';
And when I saw the turf that covered him,
After the lapse of full eight years, those words,
With sound of voice and countenance of the Man,
Came back upon me, so that some few tears
Fell from me in my own despite. And now,
Thus travelling smoothly o'er the level sands,
I thought with pleasure of the verses graven
Upon his tombstone, saying to myself:
He loved the Poets, and, if now alive,
Would have loved me, as one not destitute
Of promise, nor belying the kind hope
Which he had formed, when I, at his command,
Began to spin, at first, my toilsome songs.

RESOLUTION AND INDEPENDENCE

THERE was a roaring in the wind all night;
The rain came heavily and fell in floods;
But now the sun is rising calm and bright;
The birds are singing in the distant woods;
Over his own sweet voice the Stock-dove broods;
The Jay makes answer as the Magpie chatters;
And all the air is filled with pleasant noise of waters.

II   All things that love the sun are out of doors;
The sky rejoices in the morning's birth;
The grass is bright with rain-drops;—on the moors
The hare is running races in her mirth;
And with her feet she from the plashy earth
Raises a mist; that, glittering in the sun,
Runs with her all the way, wherever she doth run.

III   I was a Traveller then upon the moor;
I saw the hare that raced about with joy;
I heard the woods and distant waters roar;
Or heard them not, as happy as a boy:
The pleasant season did my heart employ:
My old remembrances went from me wholly;
And all the ways of men, so vain and melancholy.

IV   But, as it sometimes chanceth, from the might
Of joy in minds that can no further go,
As high as we have mounted in delight
In our dejection do we sink as low;
To me that morning did it happen so;

And fears and fancies thick upon me came;
Dim sadness—and blind thoughts, I knew not, nor could name.

v   I heard the sky-lark warbling in the sky;
And I bethought me of the playful hare:
Even such a happy Child of earth am I;
Even as these blissful creatures do I fare;
Far from the world I walk, and from all care;
But there may come another day to me—
Solitude, pain of heart, distress, and poverty.

VI   My whole life I have lived in pleasant thought,
As if life's business were a summer mood;
As if all needful things would come unsought
To genial faith, still rich in genial good;
But how can He expect that others should
Build for him, sow for him, and at his call
Love him, who for himself will take no heed at all?

VII   I thought of Chatterton, the marvellous Boy,
The sleepless Soul that perished in his pride;
Of Him who walked in glory and in joy
Following his plough, along the mountain-side:
By our own spirits are we deified:
We Poets in our youth begin in gladness;
But thereof come in the end despondency and madness.

VIII   Now, whether it were by peculiar grace,
A leading from above, a something given,
Yet it befell that, in this lonely place,
When I with these untoward thoughts had striven,
Beside a pool bare to the eye of heaven
I saw a Man before me unawares:
The oldest man he seemed that ever wore grey hairs.

[74]

IX   As a huge stone is sometimes seen to lie
Couched on the bald top of an eminence;
Wonder to all who do the same espy,
By what means it could thither come, and whence;
So that it seems a thing endued with sense:
Like a sea-beast crawled forth, that on a shelf
Of rock or sand reposeth, there to sun itself;

X   Such seemed this Man, not all alive nor dead,
Nor all asleep—in his extreme old age:
His body was bent double, feet and head
Coming together in life's pilgrimage;
As if some dire constraint of pain, or rage
Of sickness felt by him in times long past,
A more than human weight upon his frame had cast.

[75]

XI   Himself he propped, limbs, body, and pale face,
Upon a long grey staff of shaven wood:
And, still as I drew near with gentle pace,
Upon the margin of that moorish flood
Motionless as a cloud the old Man stood,
That heareth not the loud winds when they call;
And moveth all together, if at all.

XII   At length, himself unsettling, he the pond
Stirred with his staff, and fixedly did look
Upon the muddy water, which he conned,
As if he had been reading in a book:
And now a stranger's privilege I took;
And, drawing to his side, to him did say,
'This morning gives us promise of a glorious day.'

XIII   A gentle answer did the old Man make,
In courteous speech which forth he slowly drew:
And him with further words I thus bespake,
'What occupation do you there pursue?
This is a lonesome place for one like you.'
Ere he replied, a flash of mild surprise
Broke from the sable orbs of his yet-livid eyes.

XIV   His words came feebly, from a feeble chest,
But each in solemn order followed each,
With something of a lofty utterance drest—
Choice word and measured phrase, above the reach
Of ordinary men; a stately speech;
Such as grave Livers do in Scotland use,
Religious men, who give to God and man their dues.

XV   He told, that to these waters he had come
To gather leeches, being old and poor:

Employment hazardous and wearisome!
And he had many hardships to endure:
From pond to pond he roamed, from moor to moor;
Housing, with God's good help, by choice or chance;
And in this way he gained an honest maintenance.

XVI   The old Man still stood talking by my side;
But now his voice to me was like a stream
Scarce heard; nor word from word could I divide;
And the whole body of the Man did seem
Like one whom I had met with in a dream;
Or like a man from some far region sent,
To give me human strength, by apt admonishment.

XVII   My former thoughts returned: the fear that kills;
And hope that is unwilling to be fed;
Cold, pain, and labour, and all fleshly ills;
And mighty Poets in their misery dead.
—Perplexed, and longing to be comforted,
My question eagerly did I renew,
'How is it that you live, and what is it you do?'

XVIII   He with a smile did then his words repeat;
And said that, gathering leeches, far and wide
He travelled; stirring thus about his feet
The waters of the pools where they abide.
'Once I could meet with them on every side;
But they have dwindled long by slow decay;
Yet still I persevere, and find them where I may.'

XIX   While he was talking thus, the lonely place,
The old Man's shape, and speech—all troubled me:
In my mind's eye I seemed to see him pace
About the weary moors continually,
Wandering about alone and silently.
While I these thoughts within myself pursued,
He, having made a pause, the same discourse renewed.

XX   And soon with this he other matter blended,
Cheerfully uttered, with demeanour kind,
But stately in the main; and, when he ended,
I could have laughed myself to scorn to find
In that decrepit Man so firm a mind.
'God,' said I, 'be my help and stay secure;
I'll think of the Leech-gatherer on the lonely moor!'

MICHAEL

A PASTORAL POEM

IF from the public way you turn your steps
Up the tumultuous brook of Green-head Ghyll,
You will suppose that with an upright path
Your feet must struggle; in such bold ascent
The pastoral mountains front you, face to face.
But, courage! for around that boisterous brook
The mountains have all opened out themselves,
And made a hidden valley of their own.
No habitation can be seen; but they
Who journey thither find themselves alone
With a few sheep, with rocks and stones, and kites
That overhead are sailing in the sky.
It is in truth an utter solitude;
Nor should I have made mention of this Dell
But for one object which you might pass by,
Might see and notice not. Beside the brook
Appears a straggling heap of unhewn stones!
And to that simple object appertains
A story—

Upon the forest-side in Grasmere Vale
There dwelt a Shepherd, Michael was his name;
An old man, stout of heart, and strong of limb.
His bodily frame had been from youth to age
Of an unusual strength: his mind was keen,
Intense, and frugal, apt for all affairs,
And in his shepherd's calling he was prompt
And watchful more than ordinary men.
Hence had he learned the meaning of all winds,
Of blasts of every tone; and oftentimes,
When others heeded not, He heard the South
Make subterraneous music, like the noise
Of bagpipers on distant Highland hills.
The Shepherd, at such warning, of his flock
Bethought him, and he to himself would say,
'The winds are now devising work for me!'
And, truly, at all times, the storm, that drives
The traveller to a shelter, summoned him
Up to the mountains: he had been alone
Amid the heart of many thousand mists,
That came to him, and left him, on the heights.
So lived he till his eightieth year was past,
And grossly that man errs, who should suppose
That the green valleys, and the streams and rocks,
Were things indifferent to the Shepherd's thoughts.
Fields, where with cheerful spirits he had breathed
The common air; hills, which with vigorous step
He had so often climbed; which had impressed
So many incidents upon his mind
Of hardship, skill or courage, joy or fear;
Which, like a book, preserved the memory
Of the dumb animals, whom he had saved,
Had fed or sheltered, linking to such acts
The certainty of honourable gain;

[80]

Those fields, those hills—what could they less? had laid
Strong hold on his affections, were to him
A pleasurable feeling of blind love,
The pleasure which there is in life itself.

His days had not been passed in singleness.
His Helpmate was a comely matron, old—
Though younger than himself full twenty years.
She was a woman of a stirring life,
Whose heart was in her house: two wheels she had
Of antique form; this large, for spinning wool;
That small, for flax; and, if one wheel had rest,
It was because the other was at work.
The Pair had but one inmate in their house,
An only Child, who had been born to them
When Michael, telling o'er his years, began
To deem that he was old,—in shepherd's phrase,
With one foot in the grave. This only Son,
With two brave sheep-dogs tried in many a storm,
The one of an inestimable worth,
Made all their household. I may truly say,
That they were a proverb in the vale
For endless industry. When day was gone,
And from their occupations out of doors
The Son and Father were come home, even then,
Their labour did not cease; unless when all
Turned to the cleanly supper-board, and there,
Each with a mess of pottage and skimmed milk,
Sat round the basket piled with oaten cakes,
And their plain home-made cheese. Yet when the meal
Was ended, Luke (for so the Son was named)
And his old Father both betook themselves
To such convenient work as might employ
Their hands by the fire-side; perhaps to card

[82]

Wool for the Houswife's spindle, or repair
Some injury done to sickle, flail, or scythe,
Or other implement of house or field.

Thus living on through such a length of years,
The Shepherd, if he loved himself, must needs
Have loved his Helpmate; but to Michael's heart
This son of old age was yet more dear—
Less from instinctive tenderness, the same
Fond spirit that blindly works in the blood of all—
Than that a child, more than all other gifts
That earth can offer to declining man,
Brings hope with it, and forward-looking thoughts,
And stirrings of inquietude, when they
By tendency of nature needs must fail.
Exceeding was the love he bare to him,
His heart and his heart's joy! For oftentimes
Old Michael, while he was a babe in arms,
Had done him female service, not alone
For pastime and delight, as is the use
Of fathers, but with patient mind enforced
To acts of tenderness; and he had rocked
His cradle, as with a woman's gentle hand.

And when by Heaven's good grace the boy grew up
A healthy Lad, and carried in his cheek
Two steady roses that were five years old;
Then Michael from a winter coppice cut
With his own hand a sapling, which he hooped
With iron, making it throughout in all
Due requisites a perfect shepherd's staff,
And gave it to the Boy; wherewith equipt
He as a watchman oftentimes was placed
At gate or gap, to stem or turn the flock;

And, to his office prematurely called,
There stood the urchin, as you will divine,
Something between a hindrance and a help;
And for this cause not always, I believe,
Receiving from his Father hire of praise;
Though nought was left undone which staff, or voice,
Or looks, or threatening gestures, could perform.

    But soon as Luke, full ten years old, could stand
Against the mountain blasts; and to the heights,
Not fearing toil, nor length of weary ways,
He with his Father daily went, and they
Were as companions, why should I relate
That objects which the Shepherd loved before
Were dearer now? that from the Boy there came
Feelings and emanations—things which were
Light to the sun and music to the wind;
And that the old Man's heart seemed born again?

[84]

Thus in his Father's sight the Boy grew up:
And now, when he had reached his eighteenth year,
He was his comfort and his daily hope.

While in this sort the simple household lived
From day to day, to Michael's ear there came
Distressful tidings. Long before the time
Of which I speak, the Shepherd had been bound
In surety for his brother's son, a man
Of an industrious life, and ample means;
But unforeseen misfortunes suddenly
Had prest upon him; and old Michael now
Was summoned to discharge the forfeiture,
A grievous penalty, but little less
Than half his substance. This unlooked-for claim,
At the first hearing, for a moment took
More hope out of his life than he supposed
That any old man ever could have lost.
As soon as he had armed himself with strength
To look his troubles in the face, it seemed
The Shepherd's sole resource to sell at once
A portion of the patrimonial fields.
Such was his first resolve; he thought again,
And his heart failed him. 'Isabel,' said he,
Two evenings after he had heard the news,
'I have been toiling more than seventy years,
And in the open sunshine of God's love
Have we all lived; yet, if these fields of ours
Should pass into a stranger's hand, I think
That I could not lie quiet in my grave.
Our lot is a hard lot; the sun himself
Has scarcely been more diligent than I;
And I have lived to be a fool at last
To my own family. An evil man

That was, and made an evil choice, if he
Were false to us; and, if he were not false,
There are ten thousand to whom loss like this
Had been no sorrow. I forgive him;—but
'Twere better to be dumb than to talk thus.

When I began, my purpose was to speak
Of remedies and of a cheerful hope.
Our Luke shall leave us, Isabel; the land
Shall not go from us, and it shall be free;
He shall possess it, free as is the wind
That passes over it. We have, thou know'st,
Another kinsman—he will be our friend
In this distress. He is a prosperous man,
Thriving in trade—and Luke to him shall go,
And with his kinsman's help and his own thrift
He quickly will repair this loss, and then
He may return to us. If here he stay,
What can be done? Where every one is poor,
What can be gained?'
　　　At this the old Man paused,
And Isabel sat silent, for her mind
Was busy, looking back into past times.
There's Richard Bateman, thought she to herself,
He was a parish-boy—at the church-door
They made a gathering for him, shillings, pence,
And halfpennies, wherewith the neighbours bought
A basket, which they filled with pedlar's wares;
And, with this basket on his arm, the lad
Went up to London, found a master there,
Who, out of many, chose the trusty boy
To go and overlook his merchandise
Beyond the seas; where he grew wondrous rich,
And left estates and monies to the poor,

[86]

And, at his birth-place, built a chapel floored
With marble, which he sent from foreign lands.
These thoughts, and many others of like sort,
Passed quickly through the mind of Isabel,
And her face brightened. The old Man was glad,
And thus resumed:—'Well, Isabel! this scheme
These two days has been meat and drink to me.
Far more than we have lost is left us yet.
—We have enough—I wish indeed that I
Were younger;—but this hope is a good hope.
Make ready Luke's best garments, of the best
Buy for him more, and let us send him forth
To-morrow, or the next day, or to-night:
     If he *could* go, the Boy should go to-night.'

     Here Michael ceased, and to the fields went forth
With a light heart. The Housewife for five days
Was restless morn and night, and all day long
Wrought on with her best fingers to prepare
Things needful for the journey of her son.

     The expected letter from their kinsman came,
With kind assurances that he would do
His utmost for the welfare of the Boy;
To which, requests were added, that forthwith
He might be sent to him. Ten times or more
The letter was read over; Isabel
Went forth to show it to the neighbours round;
Nor was there at that time on English land
A prouder heart than Luke's. When Isabel
Had to her house returned, the old Man said,
'He shall depart to-morrow.' To this word
The Housewife answered, talking much of things
Which, if at such short notice he should go,

Would surely be forgotten. But at length
She gave consent, and Michael was at ease.

　　Near the tumultuous brook of Green-head Ghyll,
In that deep valley, Michael had designed
To build a Sheep-fold; and, before he heard
The tidings of his melancholy loss,
For this same purpose he had gathered up
A heap of stones, which by the streamlet's edge
Lay thrown together, ready for the work.
With Luke that evening thitherward he walked:
And soon as they had reached the place he stopped,
And thus the old Man spake to him:—'My son,
To-morrow thou wilt leave me: with full heart
I look upon thee, for thou art the same
That wert a promise to me ere thy birth,
And all thy life hast been my daily joy.
I will relate to thee some little part

[88]

Of our two histories; 'twill do thee good
When thou art from me, even if I should touch
On things thou canst not know of.—After thou
First cam'st into the world—as oft befalls
To new-born infants—thou didst sleep away
Two days, and blessings from thy Father's tongue
Then fell upon thee. Day by day passed on,
And still I loved thee with increasing love.
Never to living ear came sweeter sounds
Than when I heard thee by our own fire-side
First uttering, without words, a natural tune;
While thou, a feeding babe, didst in thy joy
Sing at thy Mother's breast. Month followed month,
And in the open fields my life was passed
And on the mountains; else I think that thou
Hadst been brought up upon thy Father's knees.
But we were playmates, Luke: among these hills,
As well thou knowest, in us the old and young
Have played together, nor with me didst thou
Lack any pleasure which a boy can know.'
Luke had a manly heart; but at these words
He sobbed aloud. The old Man grasped his hand,
And said, 'Nay, do not take it so—I see
That these are things of which I need not speak.
—Even to the utmost I have been to thee
A kind and a good Father: and herein
I but repay a gift which I myself
Received at others' hands; for, though now old
Beyond the common life of man, I still
Remember them who loved me in my youth.
Both of them sleep together: here they lived,
As all their Forefathers had done; and, when
At length their time was come, they were not loth
To give their bodies to the family mould.

I wished that thou shouldst live the life they lived,
But 'tis a long time to look back, my Son,
And see so little gain from threescore years.
These fields were burthened when they came to me;
Till I was forty years of age, not more
Than half of my inheritance was mine.
I toiled and toiled; God blessed me in my work,
And till these three weeks past the land was free.
—It looks as if it never could endure
Another Master. Heaven forgive me, Luke,
If I judge ill for thee, but it seems good
That thou shouldst go.'
       At this the old Man paused;
Then, pointing to the stones near which they stood,
Thus, after a short silence, he resumed:
'This was a work for us; and now, my Son,
It is a work for me. But, lay one stone—
Here, lay it for me, Luke, with thine own hands.
Nay, Boy, be of good hope;—we both may live
To see a better day. At eighty-four
I still am strong and hale;—do thou thy part;
I will do mine.—I will begin again
With many tasks that were resigned to thee:
Up to the heights, and in among the storms,
Will I without thee go again, and do
All works which I was wont to do alone,
Before I knew thy face.—Heaven bless thee, Boy!
Thy heart these two weeks has been beating fast
With many hopes; it should be so—yes—yes—
I knew that thou couldst never have a wish
To leave me, Luke: thou hast been bound to me
Only by links of love: when thou art gone,
What will be left to us!—But I forget
My purposes. Lay now the corner-stone,

As I requested; and hereafter, Luke,
When thou art gone away, should evil men
Be thy companions, think of me, my Son,
And of this moment; hither turn thy thoughts,
And God will strengthen thee: amid all fear
And all temptation, Luke, I pray that thou
May'st bear in mind the life thy Fathers lived,
Who, being innocent, did for that cause
Bestir them in good deeds. Now, fare thee well—
When thou return'st, thou in this place wilt see
A work which is not here: a covenant
'Twill be between us; but, whatever fate
Befall thee, I shall love thee to the last,
And bear thy memory with me to the grave.'

   The Shepherd ended here; and Luke stooped down,
And, as his Father had requested, laid
The first stone of the Sheep-fold. At the sight
The old Man's grief broke from him; to his heart
He pressed his Son, he kissed him and wept;
And to the house together they returned.
—Hushed was that House in peace, or seeming peace,
Ere the night fell:—with morrow's dawn the Boy
Began his journey, and, when he had reached
The public way, he put on a bold face;
And all the neighbours, as he passed their doors,
Came forth with wishes and with farewell prayers,
That followed him till he was out of sight.

   A good report did from their Kinsman come,
Of Luke and his well-doing: and the Boy
Wrote loving letters, full of wondrous news,
Which, as the Housewife phrased it, were throughout
'The prettiest letters that were ever seen.'

Both parents read them with rejoicing hearts.
So, many months passed on: and once again
The Shepherd went about his daily work
With confident and cheerful thoughts; and now
Sometimes when he could find a leisure hour
He to that valley took his way, and there
Wrought at the Sheep-fold. Meantime Luke began
To slacken in his duty; and, at length,
He in the dissolute city gave himself
To evil courses: ignominy and shame
Fell on him, so that he was driven at last
To seek a hiding-place beyond the seas.

There is a comfort in the strength of love;
'Twill make a thing endurable, which else
Would overset the brain, or break the heart:
I have conversed with more than one who well
Remember the old Man, and what he was
Years after he had heard this heavy news.
His bodily frame had been from youth to age
Of an unusual strength. Among the rocks
He went, and still looked up to sun and cloud,
And listened to the wind; and, as before,
Performed all kinds of labour for his sheep,
And for the land, his small inheritance.
And to that hollow dell from time to time
Did he repair, to build the Fold of which
His flock had need. 'Tis not forgotten yet
The pity which was then in every heart
For the old Man—and 'tis believed by all
That many and many a day he thither went,
And never lifted up a single stone.

There, by the Sheep-fold, sometimes was he seen

Sitting alone, or with his faithful Dog,
Then old, beside him, lying at his feet.
The length of full seven years, from time to time,
He at the building of this Sheep-fold wrought,
And left the work unfinished when he died.
Three years, or little more, did Isabel
Survive her Husband: at her death the estate
Was sold, and went into a stranger's hand.
The Cottage which was named *The Evening Star*
Is gone—the ploughshare has been through the ground
On which it stood; great changes have been wrought
In all the neighbourhood:—yet the oak is left
That grew beside their door; and the remains
Of the unfinished Sheep-fold may be seen
Beside the boisterous brook of Greenhead Ghyll.

AFTER-THOUGHT

I THOUGHT of Thee, my partner and my guide,
As being past away.—Vain sympathies!
For, backward, Duddon! as I cast my eyes,
I see what was, and is, and will abide;
Still glides the Stream, and shall for ever glide;
The Form remains, the Function never dies;
While we, the brave, the mighty, and the wise,
We Men, who in our morn of youth defied
The elements, must vanish;—be it so!
Enough, if something from our hands have power
To live, and act, and serve the future hour;
And if, as toward the silent tomb we go,
Through love, through hope, and faith's transcendent dower,
We feel that we are greater than we know.

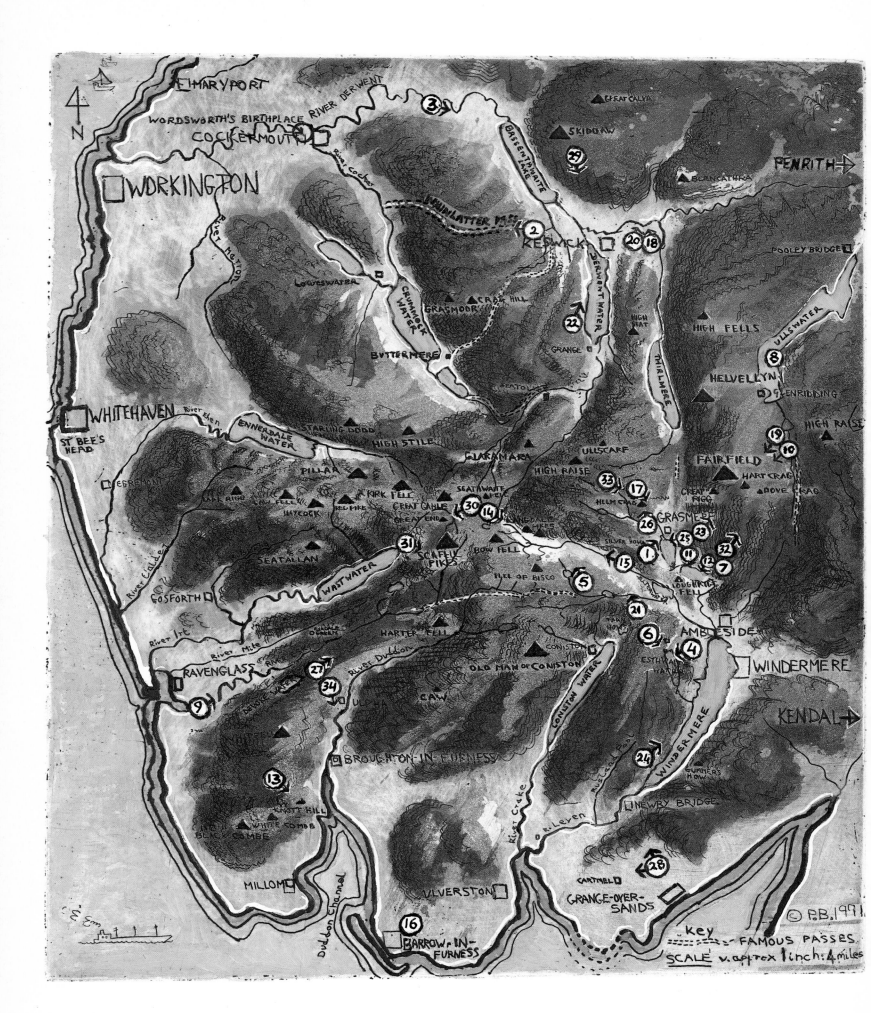

LIST OF ILLUSTRATIONS

The number in parentheses after an entry refers to the location on the map

page

i   Grasmere with Fairfield behind : high noon in June (1)

iii   In the Whinlatter Pass (2)

2   Skiddaw from the Derwent near Isel Bridge (3)
Oh, many a time have I . . . made one long bathing of a summer's day

3   Wis-een Tarn from Claiffe Heights, southern Lakeland fells in distance (4)
To range the open heights where woodcocks run

4   Hazel wood in May
The shady nook of hazels

8   The Langdale Pikes from Blea Tarn, February (5)
Ye visions of the hills! And Souls of lonely places

10   Priest Pot and Esthwaite Water, from the north (6)
The single sheep, and the one blasted tree

11   The stone summer house at Rydal Mount, built by Wordsworth (7)
And in this later time

12   Stybarrow Crag on Ullswater (8)
A huge peak, black and huge

14   On the shore of Ullswater
One summer evening led by her

18   The Esk estuary near Ravenglass, looking towards Scafell (9)
I travelled among unknown men

20   The Wye near Symonds Yat, October
O sylvan Wye! thou wanderer thro' the woods

26   The evening star above Dove Crag at the head of Dovedale (10)
She dwelt among the untrodden ways

27   Rydal Water : October afternoon (11)

28   Loughrigg Fell above Rydal Water, April (12)
I wandered lonely as a cloud

30   Waterfall, summer evening
Brook! whose society the Poet seeks

31   A medlar tree, seen by night and day, with cuckoo
And the first cuckoo's melancholy cry

32   Swinside stone circle, with sunrise behind Knott Hill (13)
Great God I'd rather be a Pagan

33   Bolton Priory from the north east, high summer
Along the banks of crystal wharf

34   Bolton Priory, July morning

35   Mickleden from Rossett Pike (14)
I turned to share the transport—Oh! with whom

36   Wren's nest in reeds
Among the dwelling framed by birds

39   A wren's nest

40-1 The Vale of Grasmere from Helm Crag (17)

42 The Langdale Pikes: October morning (15)
While not a leaf seems faded

43 Furness Abbey: the once great East Window (16)

45 Blencathra, in the distance, in March (18)
Then sing ye Birds, sing, sing a joyous song!

48 Hart Crag from near Hartsop Hall, Dovedale (19)
While the young lambs bound

52 Summer waterfall in the Lakes
I love the Brooks

54 Castlerigg stone circle and Blencathra (20)
It is the first mild day of March

55 Castle How from Tarn Hows: February evening (21)
How clear, how keen, how marvellously bright

57 Gordale Scar
Let thy feet repair To Gordale-chasm

58 Derwent Water: November the fifth (22)

60 Moon sinking between Fairfield and Rydal Fell from Dove Cottage (23)
Strange fits of passion have I known

62 Southern Windermere from 'The Brows' (24)
There was a Boy; ye knew him well, ye cliffs

64 Silver Howe from the east bank of Grasmere (25)
Clouds, lingering yet, extend in solid bars

67 May morning at Lancrigg, near Grasmere (26)
Musing in solitude, I oft perceive

69 Ash tree in spring leaf, with swallows
Paradise, and groves Elysian, Fortunate Fields

70 Harter Fell from near Devoke Water: high noon (27)
To a Skylark

72 Sunset: Cartmel to the west, the fells to the north (28)

75 Derwent Water from Carl Side, Skiddaw (29)
A huge stone is sometimes seen to lie

77 Looking past Scafell Pikes towards Wasdale: March (30)
From pond to pond he roamed, from moor to moor

79 Summer sunrise above Sca Fell from Wasdale Head (31)
He with his Father daily went

81 Haymaking, with Grasmere in the background
Green valleys, and the streams and rocks

84 Alcock Tarn from above Dove Cottage (32)
Against the mountain blasts

88 The ruined sheep-fold

93 Autumn sunrise behind Helm Crag, from Greenburn Bottom (33)
. . . the tumultuous brook

95 The Duddon estuary: sunset in August (34)
Still glides the Stream, and shall forever glide